Chard
and Ilminster

IN OLD PHOTOGRAPHS

John Stringfellow. Born at Attercliffe, Sheffield in 1799, John Stringfellow was apprenticed to the lace trade in Nottingham. He moved to Chard in 1820 and set up a factory at the house which he built in High Street and which is still standing. After some years of experimenting he produced a ten-foot model aeroplane which, by means of a steam engine, flew some forty feet under its own power. Later that year he achieved a distance of 120 feet in London. For many years he tinkered with powered flight and Chard, quite rightly, greets the visitor with 'Chard – birthplace of powered flight' on its town signs. Stringfellow died on 13 December 1883 and is buried in the cemetery at Crimchard where there is a small model of his aeroplane on the grave.

Chard
and Ilminster

IN OLD PHOTOGRAPHS

Collected by GERALD GOSLING
AND FRANK HUDDY

Budding
BOOKS

A Budding Book

This book was first published in 1992 by
Sutton Publishing Limited · Phoenix Mill
Thrupp · Stroud · Gloucestershire · GL5 2BU

This edition first published in 2001 by
Budding Books, an imprint of
Sutton Publishing Limited

Reprinted 2005

British Library Cataloguing in Publication Data
A catalogue record for this book is available from
the British Library

ISBN 1-84015-244-3

Typeset in 9/10 Sabon.
Typesetting and origination by
Sutton Publishing Limited.
Printed in Great Britain by
J.H. Haynes & Co. Ltd, Sparkford.

For our wives, Violet and Jean.

Contents

	Introduction	7
1.	Chard	9
2.	At Work ...	41
3.	... and Play	59
4.	Chard's Villages	93
5.	Ilminster Within	119
6.	Ilminster Without	145
	Acknowledgements	160

Boden's Mill, Chard, *c*.1950. Boden & Co., a family lace-making business, closed in the late 1930s. The premises were later occupied by Dualloys, plain bearing manufacturers, who became Glacier Metal Co. Ltd and moved to Winterhay Lane in Ilminster in 1973. The tall chimney was taken down on safety grounds in the early 1980s and the old mill is now small industrial units. Heather Manning is the girl on the left in the gateway, which bears the date 1901 and was the spot where boys waited when bringing food and drink for parents on late shifts.

INTRODUCTION

Chard and Ilminster, closely linked neighbours in the southernmost corner of Somerset, abound in history, and have managed to combine industry with traditional agriculture to provide the background against which the working day is passed. Chard in particular, and with some justification, is said to have had a higher percentage of its population working in factories and mills than any other place in the realm.

But Chard goes back far beyond the Industrial Revolution. The hills around are full of prehistoric man's remains. The Romans passed by, but the Saxons, who called it Cerde or Cherde after their king Cerdic, stayed. Charles I came here twice. Monmouth was greeted enthusiastically, but Judge Jeffries less so when he hanged twelve men, thankfully not Chardians, at the bottom of the town.

Chard is full of old and beautiful buildings including the fifteenth-century St Mary's church, the Guildhall, the Grammar School, formerly a private residence, Choughs Hotel, Manor Court and the Museum. The list is endless. All jostle happily with the stark, conventional shapes of the mills which have a beauty of their own, especially to the student of industrial architecture. It claims to be the highest town in Somerset and, of the two swift-moving streams that flank its wide, main street, one turns north at the bottom of the town to join the Isle and eventually reach the sea in the Bristol Channel, the other heads south for the English Channel via the River Axe.

Chard sends its products across the five continents: Phoenix Engineering alone exports to around 150 different countries. But it has done more for the world than that. Powered flight was invented here; so were artificial limbs. And one of the first blows was struck for Women's Lib when local woman Margaret Bondfield became the first of her sex to obtain Cabinet status as Minister of Labour in Ramsay McDonald's government in 1929.

Ilminster looks older than Chard. It is certainly quieter, especially since the new bypass has taken the traffic away to the north of the town. Its crowning glory is the fifteenth-century St Mary's Minster (a popular dedication in this part of Somerset), thought to have been modelled on Wells Cathedral. It has a fine south transept chapel, with outstanding brasses on the tombs of the Wadhams, including that of Nicholas who founded Wadham College, Oxford. The grammar school was once housed in the Elizabethan building beside the Minister, and Court Barton, picturesque cottages tucked away to the rear, is well worth a visit. The Unitarian chapel in East Street is said to be one of the oldest in the country and the George Hotel, a handsome coaching inn, looks out over the Square at a single-storeyed, pillared market hall. It was to the George that Queen Victoria, still in her swaddling clothes, was brought by her parents, the Duke and Duchess of Kent, just before Christmas 1819 when they were on their way to Sidmouth to escape the Duke's creditors.

Ilminster has tucked most of its industry in its northern corner and, although it makes agricultural machinery, plastics, shirts, collars and gloves among other things, and has a large dairy there, it has none of the appearance of the 'dark Satanic mill'.

Both towns are surrounded by some of Somerset's prettiest villages, all of which have a common agricultural thread running through their rich tapestries. But they are all different, varying from the quiet seclusion of upland Buckland St Mary in the high Blackdowns to Ilton, Ashill, Broadway and Horton, where the bustle of the A303 is never far away.

As a collector over many years of postcards and pictures of Chard and the surrounding district, a district in which I have worked as a fireman and which I have come to love, I welcome this book. All too often, books of old photographs are processions of street scenes that fail to bring out the story of the place, its people and their work and play. Gerald Gosling and Frank Huddy, though, have achieved just that with their book and it deserves every success.

Jeff Farley
Chard
August 1992

SECTION ONE

Chard

Chard post office, *c.*1905, on the corner of Fore Street and Holyrood Street, built around 1805 as a private residence. It became the premises of Chard printer Mr Toms and housed the post office for about 100 years. Local brewers Mitchell, Toms occupied the left hand side for a spell before moving to the premises just visible on the far left in 1902. In 1890 the second floor was the postmaster's sleeping quarters, but in 1905 a new postmaster lived off the premises. Telephones arrived in 1908 and were housed in a room on the second floor, and telegrams were to its left. The post office moved to the foot of Fore Street in the mid-1960s and the building is now a bakers shop and offices.

Robert Love, Holyrood Auction Mart, Chard, *c*.1910. Robert Love ran an extensive business in Holyrood Street, specializing in funerals, 'economically furnished in the latest style'. He was also a complete furnisher and cabinet maker, and removed household goods, 'to all parts by road, rail and sea'. The three coachmen above are, left to right: William Love, who ran his own livery stables a few doors away, Charles Love and Mr Jarvis. Jesse, another member of the family, had a motor and cycle works in Old Town, moving to Silver Street in 1912.

G. Gillingham, Family Butchers, Holyrood Street, Chard, *c*.1922. This family business ran until well after the Second World War, and there is still a butchers shop here today run by Don Harris. He would be frowned on by the public health inspectors if he exposed his meat to the dust and passing dogs in this fashion.

General Booth's visit to Chard in 1906 soon attracted a crowd in Fore Street. He is addressing them from the first car. The cart on the right has been commandeered as a vantage point; another, on the left and carrying a barrel, tries to find a way through.

Mike Thresher, who came from Ilton, signs professional forms with Bristol City for whom he played for many years. Left to right: Pat Beasley, Bristol City manager, Mike Thresher, Jack Baulch, Chard Town chairman.

Snowdon Gatehouse, Chard, *c*.1900. The single-storey toll-house, built in 1839 on the junction of the Wambrook road and the main A30, is the most photographed building in Chard if not the whole of Somerset. The wall to the left of the cottage protected a well said to be 100 feet deep. Rumours in the 1950s that the building was to be demolished brought strong opposition from locals. The section of the A30 on the left was cut in 1827 to ease the gradient.

Toll House, Tytherleigh, *c*.1945. This toll-house on the Axminster road just below the Tytherleigh Arms was demolished in the 1960s in the interests of road safety.

Centenary of the invention of the first engine-driven aeroplane by John Stringfellow. Chard has always been proud of the Stringfellow connection – and rightly so. In 1948, when the centenary was celebrated, Chard was able to welcome back its other celebrity, Margaret Bondfield. Miss Bondfield was the first woman to reach Cabinet rank when she became Minister of Labour in Ramsay McDonald's 1929 government. She is pictured here outside Stringfellow House in High Street beside the mayor, Dr A.E. Glanville. Others in the group include Mrs Glanville, Sir Handley Page, immediately behind the mayor, Town Clerk Frank Searle, who is behind Miss Bondfield, the macebearer, Police Sergeant Keate, and members of the Town Council. Sydney Major, mayor 1948-9, is extreme right.

Clarence Herbert 'Jack' Baulch was a local man who made good. Born at Tatworth in 1916, he worked as a motor mechanic at the Central Motors Garage in East Street and went on to start his own car sales business at the old Turnpike Garage on the Honiton road. From there he started the Chard & District Coaches service at the end of the Second World War. A keen sportsman with varied interests, he was best known as a director of Yeovil Town and as chairman of the Perry Street & District Football League from 1967 to 1971. For some thirty years he was connected with Chard Town FC, becoming both its president and a life member.

Chard & District Coaches, *c.*1947. One of the early coaches with Mr Press at the wheel.

Fore Street, Chard, *c.*1908. To the left can be seen part of the Crown Hotel, now the Nat West Bank. Behind the famous old houses is the Court House where Judge Jeffries is reputed to have held one of his trials in the wake of the Monmouth Rebellion.

The Ball Inn, Fore Street, Chard, *c.*1938. The thatched Ball, now the site of Woolworths, was a great favourite on market days and added an air of charm to Chard's main street. Left to right (main group): Ivor Amos, Friend Bowers, Mr Oram the landlord and his daughter, Joe North, Henry Bowers.

Henry Bowers, pictured here with his wife Harriett, was born at Aldershot in 1841, the youngest of 22 children. His father George lived to be over 100, as did his grandfather. Henry himself died in Chard in 1946 a month short of his 105th birthday. He came to Chard in 1860, setting up in business as a horse dealer, and began a paraffin distribution business delivering in Chard and neighbouring villages from nine horse-drawn wagons. His son Henry carried on the business until 1946 when it was sold to Harvey's at Ashill, now Butler Oils.

Chard police station, *c.*1948. This building in Silver Street was demolished in 1956 and the present building erected on the same site.

Holyrood Street, Chard, *c.*1935. The small-looking building centre rear was the London Inn, one of Chard's more popular inns and licensed since the seventeenth century. Around the end of the 1970s it went to make room for International Stores and is now the site of the Somerfield supermarket.

Chard Market, c. 1908. Dwindling support due to increased mobility enabling farmers to attend Taunton, Yeovil and Exeter markets led to auctioneers R.& C. Snell pulling out of the once-thriving market in 1954. Another firm, Lawrences, tried to keep it going, but after six months it closed and is now the post office and car park.

Sainsbury's General Stores in Old Town, Chard, c.1930. Mrs Sainsbury is pictured outside the shop she ran for many years until its closure in the 1950s, when it was demolished to make way for new flats and housing.

George Hotel, Chard, *c.*1898. Standing opposite the Guildhall in Fore Street and said to have been an inn since the sixteenth century, the George came into its own in the age of the stage coach. It was the premier hotel in the town and catered for most of the big functions and civic occasions. The man standing in the entrance to the passageway leading to the stables is Fred the potman, one of Chard's characters. The lower side of the hotel is now occupied by Taylor's Travel.

George Hotel invoice of September 1907 when it was still a posting house and its 'omnibus meets all trains'.

Chard Central station, 1962. The 1640 to Taunton is being loaded with mail immediately prior to departure on 26 May. With Beeching just around the corner, it is interesting to note that the rundown of a small station doomed to closure has already begun; note the untidy state of the area to the left.

Chard Town station, c.1909. A rare picture of Chard's LSWR station, at which the first train in the town arrived from Chard Road, later Chard Junction, on 8 May 1863. The LSWR reached Chard Central by a loop line but the LSWR and GWR kept aloof from each other, even to the extent of having separate signal boxes and staff. Chard Town closed on 1 January 1917, the GWR working through from Chard Central to Chard Junction. Both lines closed to passenger traffic on 10 September 1962.

Congregational church, Fore Street, Chard, *c.*1928. Said to be the largest church in the town, the building proved a liability after its erection and dedication in 1868, heating costs in such a large building being exceptionally high. Taken down for site development in 1979 and said to be unsafe, it has been replaced by shops.

Sully's Coaches, *c.*1935. Sully's operated a service to Seaton and waged a price war with the National Bus Company that is still talked about today. They lost, and eventually sold out to their rivals, who built their depot near the ground on which Sully's fleet of Dennis coaches are lined up. Sully's later went into cinema management.

Chard RDC engine driver's cabin, *c.*1922. Steamroller men lived in these vans, the stove in view just inside the door doubling for cooking and heating. Workmen, who moved from job to job, were often away for a week at a time. The number 4 indicates that this was the fourth such vehicle in the council's fleet.

The Beviss family, *c.*1920. John Bartletts Beviss, pictured here in his father's arms at the family home at the Berea, Wambrook, near Chard, was a well-known solicitor in the Chard area, as was his father William. John, who was a POW for four years during the Second World War, died in 1982. The gentleman with the beard on the left is his grandfather Abraham.

Chard War Memorial Cottage Hospital, Crewkerne Road, Chard, *c.*1930. Visiting on Sundays and Thursdays fitted in with the Sabbath and with Chard's half day, but Monday, Tuesday and Wednesday must have dragged for many patients. Closed in around 1980, it is now a retirement home.

E.H. Austin, Holyrood Street, Chard, c.1909. Austin's, an old established drapery shop which closed in the 1970s, specialized in dressmaking, millinery and gent's outfitting. At the time of the picture it was possible to purchase three pairs of stockings for 1s. 2d.

Victoria Hotel, Chard (c.1895), ideally situated between the two stations for whose trade it catered. Victoria Avenue itself was moved sideways to make way for the railway which ran along the old line of the street.

Reg Palmer, pictured here with his son Geoffrey around 1950, was born at Yarcombe in 1897 and moved to Newhouse in Chard's Drift Road around 1915, where he farmed and became a prominent property dealer until his death in 1984. His was one of the best known faces at local markets.

Chard Industrial & Provident Society Ltd, Fore Street, Chard, c.1914. The full staff, eighteen in number, has assembled on the pavement. Today the premises, much altered, are occupied by Leo's. The gas lamp above the front door was a feature of Fore Street and is remembered with affection by older residents. It was removed in the 1920s.

James Gillingham, the pioneer of artificial limbs, mostly invented by himself, was born at Chard in 1839 and learnt his trade with his mother at the Golden Boot shoe shop in High Street. He ran his company for sixty years before his death in 1924. His son Sidney and grandson Geoffrey followed in the business, which now houses the Prospect Guest House, until the early 1960s.

Fore Street, Chard alive with bunting and flags for the coronation of George VI in 1937. The post office in particular seems to have caught the mood of the moment.

Combe Street, Chard at the same time. The contrast could hardly be greater, just one flag hung outside Rose Terrace. Cambridge Terrace is on the right, the cemetery lodge and gates are in the rear. The fir trees have now been felled.

Chard Agricultural Society Dinner, 1956. Local MP John Peyton, hands folded, with members. To his left is the society chairman, Major Jimmy Cull; Queenie and Martin Hocken are extreme right. Others in the picture include Fred McMillan, Doris Broad and Miss Luxton.

Chard Fire Brigade, c.1945. Auxiliary firemen are included. Front row, left to right: M. Summers, B. Turner, T.B. Scott, W. Summers, C. Melhuish, E. Crouch, A. Watts, M. Summers, M. Melhuish.

Charles Edward Small (*c*.1914) died a victim of the flu epidemic on 2 February 1919 aged 45 years. He was the owner of the Perry Street Lace Works, served on the Chard Board of Governors and the RDC and was chairman of Chard Parish Council. He married late in life, in 1916, Miss Elsie Dening, a member of Chard's Crimchard engineering family. But it is for his love of sport that he is best remembered today. He was a keen member of and scorer for Chard Cricket Club and a generous patron to his own works football and cricket teams. In 1903 he was responsible for the formation of the Perry Street & District Football League, then with five teams, today with over sixty. Charles Small was the league's first president and the presidency stayed in the Small family until 1983, Charles being followed in office by his nephew John, his widow Elsie, his niece Vera and, from 1983, by the league's long-serving secretary Vic Muggeridge.

Central Motor Works, East Street, Chard, *c*.1934. Although much altered, the garage is still operating opposite the junction with Furnham Road. Left to right: Jack Baulch, Jim Gilpin, Doug Hallett.

Beer & Sons, c.1908. An old-established Chard firm by the time of this picture, having been in lower Fore Street since 1878, Beer's were hairdressers for both sexes, sold fancy goods and were tobacconists. They had a high reputation in the latter field with their Chard Mixture and Cotley Hunt Mixture, both selling at around 5d. per ounce. Today Thresher's Drink Store occupies the premises.

E.J. Cuff, 1916. Cuff's shop on the corner of Fore Street and Boden Street supplied most of the local gentry and farmers with their equestrian requirements. Much of the harness was made on the premises and, besides whips, bridles, spurs and so forth, all kinds of bags, portmanteaux and trunks were stocked and repaired. Long & Bartlett still sell leather goods here.

Masters, High Street, Chard, *c*.1912.

B. Thorne & Co., High Street, Chard, *c*.1910. Thorne's were drapers of some repute and covered a wide area in Somerset and Devon. They used this view of their premises as an advertisement on cards sent to customers. This card went to a Mr Baker at Otterton, some thirty miles from Chard, to tell him that Mr Thorne would call at 8.45 a.m. on Thursday. The premises are now occupied by Chard Conservative Club.

Chard School, c.1898. The school was founded in 1671 in a building erected as a private residence in 1583. Today it is a private school. The lamp standard, for so long one of Chard's landmarks and erected to mark Queen Victoria's Diamond Jubilee, was sadly demolished in the 1950s for road safety. A trough placed beside it in 1903 to mark the death of William Hussey while trying to save Ernie James from drowning in Chard Reservoir was taken and placed in Millfield.

Fore Street, Chard, c.1908. The building with the flagpole is Chard Liberal Club, now the Working Men's Club. The stone wall at the beginning of East Street is now the RS Cars fuel station. Clarke's delivery van ambles towards it.

Press & Co., Fore Street, Chard. Press & Co., the Cornhill Motor & Cycle Works, who had a branch in East Street, Ilminster in the very early years of the twentieth century, supplied just about everything the motorist and cyclist needed, and could have cycles made to the customer's own specifications. An idea of the wages paid at the time can be had from one of their invoices which, with taxi mileage charges, has, 'waiting two hours, two shillings and sixpence'. Norrington's shop later occupied this site for many years.

Jarman & Co., Nurserymen, East Street, Chard, *c.*1904. Jarman's, who ceased trading in the 1970s when much of their nursery area went for development, had nurseries on both the Crewkerne and the Honiton roads. They were owned at the time of the photograph by Mr A.E. Townsend who was to become Chard's mayor in 1905-06 and 1923-26. The workmen cleaning the drains are using a force pump made locally at the Phoenix Engineering Works.

Fore Street, Chard, *c.*1902. With the bottom end of Fore Street and Chard School in the background, a horse-drawn refuse cart made by Phoenix Engineering is taken to Chard Town station for delivery to Warrington Corporation Highway Department.

Knight's Farm, Crimchard, Chard, c.1922. The farm was below Dening's Crimchard factory, just above the new entrance to the modern Glynswood estate, and never rebuilt after it was burnt down around 1927.

Chard branch of the National Farmers' Union on a visit to Seal-Hayne College in May 1936.

Choughs Hotel, High Street, Chard, c.1931. High Street, the continuation of Fore Street above the town centre, was not so well favoured by early photographers, which was a pity as it contained such fine old buildings as the Choughs. The hotel dates from around 1600 and, apart from the signs and porch, is little changed today. The five-light mullioned window is particularly pleasing. The 1928 Singer on the right belonged to local tailor Sammy Tutcher.

Fore Street, Chard, c.1938. There is still one horse-drawn vehicle in sight but the car has taken over now. Of interest are the Crown Hotel and the old Manor House. Boots have moved sideways to the Crown while the Manor is shops and offices. On the skyline to the left is the spire of the Congregational church; to the right, the Guildhall clock. The Guildhall, built in 1834 on the site of an early building, stands out into the street with a two-storey portico, Tuscan columns, pediment and a wooden lantern.

Ship Inn, Furnham Road, Chard, *c*.1919, another part of the town seldom photographed. The road here, especially Hornsbury Hill in the background, has been considerably widened. Hornsbury Hill itself was open common until it was enclosed in 1819.

Crimchard, Chard, *c*.1930. The thatched cottage standing out from the left hand line was pulled down to make room for expansion by Dening's factory slightly further up the road on the right. This part of Dening's closed through financial difficulties in 1949 and was occupied for many years by Anthony Allen. 'Cronchie' Hitchcock, one of Chard's characters, lived in the nearest house on the left..

Chard Canal was one of the last main line canals to be built in England and had a working life of just twenty-five years before it was closed by the Bristol and Exeter Railway who had bought it for £5,000. Chard Reservoir on the Chaffcombe Road was built to supply the canal. In 1925, after mixing and selling poultry food in Ilminster for two years, Mr B.G. Wyatt rented two of the old warehouses in the canal basin. He bought them in 1940 and bridged and filled the canal. After the war new silos and plant were installed. Dalgety bought the business in 1973 and spent over £1,000,000 on further modernization in 1981. This aerial view of Wyatt's plant in the old basin also shows Chard Central station, the open land behind which is now extensively developed.

Combe Street, Chard, *c*.1904. The open space in front of Rose Terrace is still part of the Phoenix Engineering Company's factory. On show here is one of their night soil boxes.

German bombs dropped beside Park Terrace in Chard during the Second World War. Happily, none of them exploded. Local legend has it that they were sabotaged by forced Czech labour.

Cotley Harriers, *c.*1882. One of the oldest pictures of the local hunt at Cotley House, the occasion and the people unknown.

SECTION TWO

At Work . . .

Chard Town station, *c.*1948, with a Dening of Chard implement ready for loading.

Small & Tidmus, now Swiss Lace, Perry Street Works, *c.*1950. This aerial view was taken before the demolition of the row of cottages in front of the lake. To locals, the lake was always called 'the pond'.

Wilts United Dairies Ltd, Chard Junction (*c.*1939), built in 1935. In spite of being bombed during the war, Wilts United attracted even Soviet attention on 11 June 1958 when it produced a then world-record 104 tons of butter in one day. The new factory dwarfs the older Salter and Stokes creamery behind, which was bought by Wilts United.

Chard Town station. A goods train loaded with trucks made by Phoenix Engineering. The goods are said to be on their way to India to help construct roads for the 1911 Durbar. If so the picture is of around 1910.

Same station, same theme, but nearly forty years later in 1947. This time the entire staff at Chard Town turn out to see off a consignment of agricultural machinery from Dening of Chard for Argentina. Dening's works manager Bill Smythe is third from right, and the station master Mr Elliott is to his left. Others include 'Wavey' Webber, Mr Green, Mr Goodfriend and Mr Larcombe.

Will Edwards and his wife Mary of the Windwhistle Inn near Cricket St Thomas. Most country inns of that time (*c*.1922) had a smallholding to supplement their often meagre trade and to provide food for customers. The Edwardses seem to have diversified more than most, with cows, a horse, turkeys, geese, ducks and chicken.

Mildred Tucker at Coombes Farm, Wambrook, *c*.1935.

Buckland St Mary Rectory, *c.*1905. Workmen posing during the building of the new rectory for the Revd Arthur Porcher Lance include Fred Matravers, a stonemason, second from right, and Arthur Grabham of Blackwater, fifth from left.

Lamb and Flag Inn, Buckland St Mary, *c.*1902. The pub had a complete facelift when the balcony was added.

Chard RDC obtained its first steam engine in 1919, a Marshall, hence the name, *Marshall No. 1*, on the name board. Gilbert Spurdle of Winsham drove it for fifteen years, collecting stone from local quarries and crushing it on site at the many road improvement schemes the RDC undertook at that time.

Chard RDC needed a considerable workforce for the road schemes. Those pictured have a board marked 'Winsham Tar Gang' but they worked all over the RDC's territory. The horse was never too tightly harnessed in case of fire. Back, left to right: Ted Dunford, Harry Chubb, Jack Butler, Tom Miller, Reg Grabham, Charles Spurdle, Ern Miller, George Martin. Front: Reg Spurdle, George Chubb, Charles Beer, William Webber.

Yonder Hill Saw Mills, a subsidiary of Salter & Stokes at Chard Junction. Hauling timber with one of the first steam tractors, of around 1922, driven by Tom Robbins.

Chard RDC steam tractor, *c.*1918. Then as now an accident soon attracts a crowd. With the tractor in the ditch near the Eagle Tavern on the main A303 road, landlord Mr Hockey, standing in front of the funnel, offers advice and, hopefully, refreshments.

Charles Dening ran an ironmongery and grocers business in Chard. Around 1865 he joined forces with John Wightman from nearby Lidmarsh to form Wightman and Dening, agricultural machinery manufacturers in Old Town. The firm changed its name to Dening & Co. and moved to Crimchard around 1881. The Dening family ran the business until 1937 but their successors, trading as Dening of Chard, ran into financial trouble and ceased trading in 1950. The picture is of the stand they took to early agricultural shows. Henry Dening is leaning on his cane, George Warren is third from left.

Dening of Chard, c.1949. Among the workforce seen here are Bert Read, George Saunders, Kath Ryan, Win Peadon, Ethel Hopkins, Grace Hoare, Vera Morgan, Alfie Tett, George Adams and Kathy Scott.

Dening of Chard, 1948. A batch of seed drills at Dening's bottom works wait to be loaded on railway wagons. Other implements give some idea of the range the firm covered. In the background are Chester Terrace and Creed's (now Fred Hole's) garage.

The Cattle Canteen, designed by Bill Bennett, assistant works manager at Dening of Chard, with the hill farmer in mind. It carried water and fodder to upland stock. Note the salt licks at the side.

Thomas John Jennings formed the Phoenix Engineering Company in November 1891 after buying the 52-year-old Phoenix Iron Works in Combe Street. By the end of the first decade of the twentieth century, the company had registered patents for, 'machines for spreading tar, etc. over road surfaces'. Four generations later the Jennings family still own and run the company on the same site and have established a reputation for leadership in the design and production of road surfacing machinery. Their products are used in over 150 countries.

Chard Gas Works, *c.*1904. Gas pipes are being laid from the gasworks under construction. The workman pumping out the trench is using a sludge pump made locally by Phoenix Engineerng.

Phoenix Engineering Works, Combe Street, Chard, *c.*1902. A workman in the yard demonstrates a force pump, one of the firm's best selling lines at the time.

Dening of Chard switched to war work during the Second World War. Here is a display of the varieties of ammunition they made.

Chardstock, *c.*1913. The English countryside was already changing out of all recognition at the end of the nineteenth century when Thomas Hardy wrote of it, 'this will go on the same tho' dynasties pass'. But some things never change, including a hard-earned drink taken by Frank Larcombe to a worker in the fields near the church.

Mill Hill sheepwash, near Chardstock, *c.*1920. The group seen here in the workers' 'uniform' include, in the front row, Walter Larcombe, Eddie Apsey and Bill Fowler.

Thrashing at Venn's Farm, Chard, *c.*1900. Today's health and safety inspectors would have plenty to say about the unguarded belts and pulleys on the machine.

Chard & District Agricultural Society, 1952. The society was well known for its high standards in ploughing. A competitor checks everything is in order before starting.

G.T. Chubb & Sons of Chardstock were responsible for building over 1,000 houses in post-war Chard. The firm was founded in 1918 by George Chubb, a wheelwright from Bewley Down. He died in 1951 aged 58 and was followed in the business by three of his sons. The firm closed as recently as 1987. The 1948 workforce at one of their many sites in Chard is, back row, left to right: Charles Chubb, Alby Larcombe, Tony Spiller, Doug French, Don Denslow, Bill Allen, Syd Chubb, George Chubb. Kneeling: Charles Sampson, Dick Chubb, Jim Chubb.

Yonder Hill 'Timber Fellers'. Some of the workers at Yonder Hill Saw Mills, Chard Junction, 1941. Standing, left to right: -?-, -?-, Les Rowe, Edward Lacey, Jim Evans, Charles Waring, Charles Beer, Harry Singleton, Harold White, George Bevin. Seated: Reg Singleton, Pat Wheaton, George Pennecar, Ted Evans, George Martin, William Lacey. On the ground: Will Long, 'Sergeant' Lacey.

'Old Moses', *c.*1900. Moses Coombes (centre), 'Old Moses' to the locals, was as much a part of Tatworth's postcard industry as the school and mills. He earned a living ditching and labouring.

John Madge, besides being a well known architect and mayor of Chard from 1921 to 1922, was a gifted water diviner and as such was in demand over a wide area. At the scene of one of his discoveries around 1930 are, left to right: Phil Webb, Chard Borough Surveyor, John Madge, the unknown landowner, and Leslie Pattemore, secretary to the Perry Street & District Football League, 1931-9.

Dening of Chard, *c.*1939. The street sign behind, 'Wharfdale Road N1', suggests this ERF belonging to the Dening fleet was in London when this was taken.

Chard & District Coaches, 1948, at an early home in the former US army camp on Furnham Road, now the Furzehill council estate.

Pudleigh Cloth Mills, Wadeford, near Chard, c.1905, was the last of the Chard cloth mills, ceasing trading in the late nineteenth century. Now partially demolished, it houses a fish farm. The Brown family of Chardleigh Green began the business around 1780, making stout cloth to high standards, and continued to trade throughout the nineteenth century.

Dualloys, 1st Machine Shop, Chard, 1950. Dualloys employed 315 people in their two machine shops at the time. Among the workers here are Syd Hill, checking the set of the bearings on the front bench, Roy Haste, Jack Swann, Irene Bide, and Harry Howes, the chargehand in the white coat at the back.

Simeon Trott, c.1922. Pictured at his coal yard with Leonard Larcombe (right), 'Sim' Trott took over the derelict coal yard in the old canal basin which had been in the hands of a Mr Gulliver at one time. When Trott retired Larcombe took over the business, which he ran until the 1950s. The Ford Model T one-ton truck was Trott's first venture into mechanized delivery.

Chard Fire Brigade, Somerset Cup winners, c.1958. Left to right: E. Crouch, A. Case, E. Tratt, A. Garrett, F. Hayball, S. Male, Station Officer S.G. Melhuish.

SECTION THREE

. . . and Play

Easter Sunday, 1911 in Chard. For many years it was traditional for Chard Band to play on the Corn Exchange following the Mayor's Parade on Easter Sunday. The ladies at Ascot had nothing on those of Chard when it came to hats.

Buckland St Mary outing, *c.*1922. The driver, seated on the left, is Mr Patten of Ilminster. Next to him are Mrs Gent, Mr Gent, Mrs T. Every, Mrs T. Watts, Miss Drake, Mrs Gist and Mrs Lewis from the Eagle Tavern. Standing: Mrs F. Collins, Mrs Newton and Miss Rose Tucker.

Buckland St Mary choir outing, *c.*1930. The driver from Sully's Coaches on the left is Fred Lee. In the back row under the 'P' of Private is Mr Jenkins of Buckland Mill, the Revd Gerald Hickman (rector 1926-31), and Fred Doble wearing a flat cap. Wearing a bowler hat is the village baker Mr Watts. The front row includes John Wyatt, Ken Gready and J. Every.

Chard Carnival, 1926. The Carnival King tableau lines up in Silver Street. Left to right: Madge Lee, Archie Boyland, Doug Hallett (the king behind), Ronald Barnes, Freda Hallett, Jack Hallett and Harold Hoskins.

Plough Sunday, St Mary's church, Buckland St Mary, 1947. The choir pose prior to the service. Mr and Mrs Sam Gready, standing by the horse's head, provided the plough for Mr H. Culmstock. Mr J. Every is standing by the tree.

Senior girls at Chard West End School, *c.*1910.

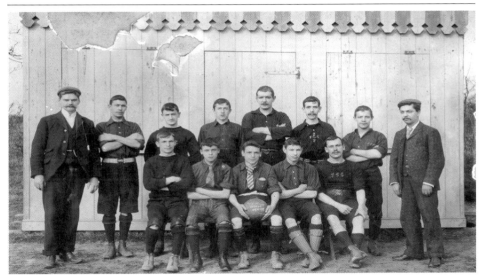

Perry Street Works Football Club, 1898/99. In 1904 this team became the first ever champions of the Perry Street & District League. Charles Small, the mill owner complete with watch, is the referee. The variety of kit is astonishing: natty trousers, shirts, Boy Scout-type belts, ties and shin pads as big as a wicket keeper's. Back row, left to right: Charles Small, L. Chambers, T. Down, W. Larcombe, J. White, W. Jerrett, S. Harris, F. Phelps (works manager). Front row: F. Bowditch, T. Bowditch, E. Cockram, C. Morris, C. Wellman.

Perry Street United Football Club, 1925/6. The United were formed out of the old Perry Street Works and the Yonder Hill Saw Mills teams in 1922-3 and, apart from two seasons, have always been members of the Perry Street & District League. Back row, left to right: L. Holman, H. Woolcott, L. Hallett, C. Harris (capt.), G. Churchill, H. Warne, A. Wells (secretary). Middle row: F. Bodger, E. Brewer, L. Chambers (chairman), A. Larcombe, T. White, R. Best (trainer). Front row: W. White, L. Churchill, G. Meech, G. Barrett, L. Brewer, F. Bilyard.

Unigate Dairies Skittle Team, Chard Junction, 1957. Back row, left to right: Ernie Hurford, Gerald Huddy, Jack Mitchell, Eddy Guppy, -?-. Front row: Bob Huddy, Ernie Long, Jack Hicks, Fred Brewer, Geoff Stone.

Chard Rugby Club, 1968. The club bought an ex-RAF hut from the camp at Melksham and the members erecting it at Chard are, left to right: Bill Lawrence, Ray Mear, Graham Salter, Bill Golesworthy, Alan Chick (behind), Ian Harris, Allan Day (behind), Jack Harris, -?-, Mike Jeffrey.

Chard Hospital Bazaar, 1906. A mixed bag on this stall outside the Liberal Club at the foot of Fore Street includes rabbits, poultry, pots and pans and bric-a-brac.

High Street, Chard, c.1890. A school procession wends its way down towards the town centre. On a wet day the ladies' long skirts would not mix too well with the muddy road. Buckland's shop behind later became Thorne's drapers and is now the Conservative Club.

Chard Carnival, 1897. The Chard Co-operative Society's tableau in the trade section offers a 2s. dividend. The balcony of the Victoria Hotel is in the background.

Bartlett's Minstrel Troop in the Guildhall for the 1907 carnival. Standing at the back, left to right: F.G. Higgins, W.H. Bartlett, S. Poole. Sitting: J. Hallett, C. Arscott, W.L. Larcombe, Mr Ireland, Mr Harvey, Mr Newbery, G. Hancock. Mr Jenkins, H. Ashford, W. Blackmore, H. Bartlett, F. Luxton, E.S. Snell, F. Hiscox, Mr Goodland.

The Diploma Dance Band at the Christmas party at Wilts United, Chard Junction, c.1946. Included are: Roy Frecknell (trumpet), Ivor Hyde (accordion), Cyril Sawyer (drummer), Dick Crick (sax). Others include the conductor Oliver Lillington, Henry Somers, Gilbert Huddy, Bob Huddy and Ben Walden.

Chardstock Mothers' Union Outing, c.1926. The destination is unknown but the ladies are off in a coach belonging to William Love. The driver, who worked for Love at his Holyrood Livery Stables in Chard (see p. 10), is splendidly unconcerned at the thought of escorting twenty ladies around. Love had served the area with horse-drawn vehicles before the war, supplying every need from weddings to funerals. By the 1920s he had moved into the motor age. Included in the group are Mrs Maude Apsey, the Chardstock postmistress, Emily Larcombe and Liz Pearce.

Tatworth Common Sports, 1952. Anthony Lillington and Ruby Rees, later Ruby Madge, receive their trophies from Eddy Wheaton, a well known local cattle dealer.

Chardstock Cricket Club, 1923. The side are pictured on their old Stoney Chilcott ground. They moved next door to their present home in 1929. During that winter a gale blew the pavilion down, lifting it over the hedge into the new home. A classic example of an ill wind. Back row, left to right: Frank Larcombe, Jack Parris, Richard Parris, Albert 'Jolly' Hutchings, Ben Parris. Middle: Alec Lisle-Smith, -?-, Alb Goff (capt.), Syd Goff, Tom Parris. Front: Harry Ithell, Neil Harris.

1st Chard Troop Baden-Powell Scouts, formed in February 1917 and pictured at camp in Charmouth in August of that year. The Scout Master, centre with legs crossed, was Mr H.W. Capern, his assistant was Revd G. Reed, centre wth arms on knees. Boys sitting, left to right: Philip Munden, Cyril Peak, Leslie Beasley, Arthur Clark, Bert Hussey, Billy Bowden, Henry Cummings, George Cummings, R. Hussey, A. Woolcott. The troop's first HQ was in Bath Street. They moved to the old community centre in Park Lane, then to Chard School and then to their present home at the Phyllis Bowers Memorial Hall.

1st Company Chard Girl Guides, 1953. Back row, left to right: -?-, Angela Baulch, Bettina Ash, Wendy Hounsell, Jennifer Pinkett, Angela Potter, Margaret Cousins, Tina Flexmore, -?-, Rita Follett, Mary Hounsell, Gillian Matthews, Pauline Woolcott. Centre: Sheila Pattemore, Mrs Marks, Edna Minson, Ann Hounsell. The front row includes Madeline Pring, fifth from left, Sheila Brown, on her left, and Susan Hopkins, end right.

Tatworth Lane, Chard, *c.*1920. Chard was full of football pitches before World War One; there were four in Union Lane alone where the Boden's works team played. Later they moved to School Lane and then Tatworth Lane. This game is being played on Bonfire Close around 1920, when it was still common for the 'bigger' games to attract four-figure gates. In 1920/21, when Boden's lost 4-2 to Axminster in the first Chard Hospital Cup Final, there were 2,534 spectators at the old Holyrood Mill ground in Mintons Lane.

Boden & Co. Football Club, 1908/9. Most of the Chard mills ran football teams and Boden's were the most successful, finishing 1st, 1st, 1st, 2nd, 3rd and 3rd in the six years prior to World War One. In this game they beat Combe St Nicholas 1-0 with a 'Jakey' Miller penalty in a play-off to win their first title. Back row, left to right: Gregory, Dowell, Coles, House, E. Hancock, A. Follett, Miller (capt.), Poole, Halse, Follett, Kirby. One thousand fans watched the game.

Chard Cricket Club, 1931. The team was unbeaten that summer, winning twenty-three of its twenty-eight games and drawing the rest. Back row, left to right: E. Harriman, R. Rooks (professional), T.B. Scott, G. Gillingham, H.L. Gollup, A. Larcombe, D. Golesworthy, S. Rowe, L. Passmore. Middle row: H.W. Larcombe, H.E. Dening (capt.), E.A. Dening. Front row: W. Coles, A. Lawrence, C.H. Lawrence, A.E. Larcombe.

Chard cricket pavilion, c.1920. The scorebox in the roof was a feature of the pavilion which had cost £98 to build in 1901. It was destroyed by an arsonist in 1961. The elm trees behind were taken down in the late 1930s.

Ada Quick, Chard Carnival Queen in 1937.

Chard Carnival, *c.*1902. Collectors line up in front of one of the floats in the station approach off Victoria Avenue, with the long platform roof of Chard Central station behind.

Alderman Ernest Ashman (mayor 1950-1) performs the crowning ceremony for the 1952 Chard Carnival. Mrs Ashman is extreme left. Joan Lilley, now Joan Oliver, is the queen, with Kay Sawyer (right) and Barbara Cosway her attendants. The Southern National Bus office behind is now Balfour News. Alderman Ashman is holding the queen's 'key' which bears the names of all previous queens and is topped with the Borough Seal. The seal is neither a crest nor a coat-of-arms and bears the date 1570, thought to be the date a new seal was cut. Chard's original charter dates from 1235.

St Mary's Church Lads Brigade at camp, *c.*1919. Leslie Pattemore is second from right.

Crimchard Mission Room Harvest Home, 1913. A fine display but who grew the bananas?

Winsham Coronation Band, 1952. The Winsham band, formed to mark Edward VII's coronation in 1902, were always great favourites at local carnivals and are gathered here for a Golden Jubilee photograph. Bert Spurdle, fourth from right in the second row from the back, was still playing the baritone horn in June 1992 when he celebrated his 91st birthday. The bandmaster in the front row is Stan Carter; to his right is Charles Phelps, a former bandmaster.

L Company 2nd Somerset (Chard) Volunteer Band, June 1882.

Perry Street Works Band, c.1900.

Chard Town Band pose in the Guildhall after the Mayor's Parade on Easter Sunday 1930. Herbert Dening (mayor 1927-32) is seated centre; also in picture are Ernest Phelps (mayor 1944-5 and 1958-9) second left, Alderman William Dominy (mayor in 1916, and who lived to be 104) fourth left front, and a former bandmaster, Fred Morris, second right. Bandsmen include Syd Cane, Bill Lewis, Fred Follett, Jim Galpin, Jack Tratt and Ben Pavey.

Chard Band, 1957. Still an all-male preserve, it would be another seven years before the first girl, Penny Bartlett, joined the ranks. Back row, left to right: Syd Cane, Alan Galpin, Howard Evans, Martin Huish, Bill Lee, John Cane, Eddie Hodges. Middle row: Jim Galpin, Roger Galpin, Rex Hounsell, Mike Chant, Reg Down, George Whaites, Bill Gardner. Front row: Bill Mico, Ron Board, Charlie Phelps (bandmaster), Dixie Dean, Jack Chubb.

Winsham School children and parents on a trip down the River Dart around 1947 include Miss Harding, a teacher, Betty Long, Mrs Warren, Christopher Warren, Mrs Down, Flossie King, Mrs Good, Ruby Dore, Margaret Dorse and Ethel Spurdle.

Bishopswood School, c.1900. Judging by the well-groomed appearence of the children, one with a Union Jack and several with mugs, this is a picture taken during the celebrations for either Queen Victoria's Diamond Jubilee or Edward VII's coronation.

Cotley Harriers at Tytherleigh Arms, *c*.1905. Hunt Master Ned Eames on the white horse would hardly look as safe today on the busy Chard–Axminster road. The Cotley Hunt was started in 1796 by Thomas Deane.

The Cotley outside the Chard Road Hotel in 1902. Like so many similar hotels, Chard Road was built to cater for the railway trade that arrived when Chard Junction opposite was built. Unlike many such places, it has survived into the post-Beeching age, albeit with a change of name to Three Counties.

Buckland St Mary Cricket Club, *c*.1910. Village matches were invariably low-scoring affairs, and no wonder with pitches as rough as this. The vicar is Revd Arthur Porcher Lance, next to him is Sam Gready, next to him the umpire, Fred Grabham. In front of Grabham is George Every, while the man with the pads is Harry Jeffery, presumably the wicket keeper.

Chard School vs Chardstock, 10 July 1954. Among the Chardstock players are George Harris, Frank Huddy, Michael Eames, Donald Goff, Arthur Larcombe, Pat Hastings and Tom Strawbridge. The School players include P. Gant, J. Alford and J. Coombes.

Chard Cricket Ground, 1904. The cricket club was formed in 1841, which makes it one of the oldest in the West Country. A large crowd has gathered to watch the match against the Nottinghamshire County side brought down most years by Charles Small. The club moved to the George ground in 1883 where the pavilion (see p. 71) was built in 1901. The Guildhall clock stands above the background of Fore Street houses.

Yuletide Bazaar in the Guildhall in 1913, attended by Mayor Edward Gawler and the mayoress.

Chard Harmonic Society giving a concert in the Guildhall in 1909. The window behind is now blocked in.

Furnham church outing to Weston-super-Mare, *c.*1910. A professional photographer always used this spot for group pictures at Weston, employing the same ledges over and over again to give his work a casual look.

Furnham Church School Treat, *c.*1907. The procession, heading for a field past Norns Terrace, has just left the church on the corner of East Street and Furnham Road.

Dualloys workers line up in Boden Street opposite the library before leaving for their 1951 outing to Weston-super-Mare in Bedford buses belonging to Victory Coaches of Horton. Those present include Pearl Greenway, Len Owsley, Bet Harris, Flo Dillan, Ed Miller, Cath Ryan and Bob Blackmore.

Tatworth School Christmas party, *c*.1947. Among the children are Sid Roulstone, Patrick Scott, Lionel Bowditch, Frank Huddy, Ruby Long, Sheila Martin, Mike Passmore, Ray Churchill, Jackie Best, Ann Kettle, Clodagh Everett and Mary Woolcott. The helpers include Vera Sweetland, Aubrey Searle, Dennis Davis, Bob Pallister and Gerald Quick.

Chard Thursday Football Club, 1907/8. With so many of Chard's workforce engaged in the retail trade, the midweek half day was the only opportunity many young men had for sport. Hence the formation of many local teams with a Wednesday or Thursday tagged on to their name. Chard's half day has long since changed from Thursday to Wednesday.

Holyrood Mills Football Club, 1912/13. The Mills played in Union Lane on what was said to be the best ground in the district and the gift of Colonel Gifford, the mill owner. Back row, left to right (players only): A. Pinney, J. Dampier, J. Hockey. Middle row: E. Jewell, V. Cook, G. Kerle. Front row: F. White, W. Beaviss, T. Kerle, W. Stacey, W. Long.

Chard Town Football Club, 1930/1. The Town club was formed in March 1921 'to represent the whole town' and, after a disastrous spell in the Somerset Senior League, joined the Perry Street & District League where, if never cutting much ice, it stayed until rejoining Somerset Senior circles in 1949. Its formation was the death knell of the mill teams who dropped out one by one. Players include: Bert Scott, fourth left in back, Kelvin Lilley (capt.), with the ball, and, in the front, Bill Coles and Tom Phippen.

Chard Town Football Club, c.1950. Back row, left to right: Ron Amos, Diddle Fowler, Charlie Smith, Bill Wyatt, Bernard Bush, Dennis Harrison. Front row: Ken Miller, Denny Hamilton, Tommy Charles, Don Harris, Ginger Cox.

Chard Town Band, *c*.1902. King Edward VII's coronation is probably the occasion for the band's playing outside Holyrood Mills in Chard. The young man in short trousers in front is Reginald Dunster, who went on to become bandmaster of Winsham Coronation Band, which was formed at this time. To his right is Jack Hill.

Buckland St Mary Girls' Friendly Society, *c*.1958. Left to right: Heather Moore, June Bodger, Mary Mitchell, Diana Hayman, Eileen Mutter (in front), Maureen Brown (behind), Susan Horner, Brenda Stokes, Ann White (in front), Margaret Scott (behind), Margaret Flaherty, Pamela Spiller, Angela Every, Kathleen Every, Valerie Bateman, Kathleen Flaherty.

Winsham Football Club, 1933/4. Back row, left to right: Charlie Beer, G. Lacey, Gilbert Spurdle, Reg Singleton, T. Bishop. Middle row: T. Evans, Billy Beer, C. Lyne. Front row: L. Long, A. Evans, F. Butler, Les Singleton, C. Spurdle.

Perry Street United Football Club. The 1950/1 team who won the Crewkerne British Legion Cup. Back row, left to right: Redvers Best, Ron Gage, Reg Bennett, Hedley Morgan, Osmond Hill, Danny Dowell, Harold Culverwell. Front row: Maurice Gage, Derek Best, Tony Hayson, B. Wakelin, Kelvin Lilly. Mascot: L. Gage.

Wambrook Sunday School visit Oren House, now Wambrook House, for tea, *c.*1910.

Bell ringers at Buckland St Mary, *c.*1914.

Chard Rugby Club was formed in 1876, which makes it one of the oldest sporting bodies in the town. Today they own their Park Road ground. The team is pictured here in around 1896.

Perry Street Cricket Club, 1948. The loss of their ground to intended factory expansion in the late 1960s spelt the death knell of the club. They tried playing all their games away but, sadly, one of the oldest local village teams is no longer with us. The 1948 side includes Harry Ithell (scorer). Ithell was professional with Chard from 1906 to 1910. Back row, left to right: Harry Ithell, Frank Buller, John Cockram, Stan Larcombe, Dave Everett, Cecil Larcombe, Fred Hoskins (umpire), Charlie Legg. Front row: Furley Mellor, Bill Steers, Doug Hallett, Nobby Larcombe, Nobby Crouch, Derek Best, Gilbert Hoare.

Guildhall, Chard, *c.*1910. This unknown occasion, with an obvious missionary theme, has packed the old Guildhall. The construction of the hall supported local industry: the pillars holdng up the tall roof were cast at Hockey's foundry in nearby East Street.

A Dening outing to see Yeovil Town lose 8-0 away to Manchester United in the FA Cup fifth round in 1949. Among those about to make the overnight trip are Jack Baulch, Bill Edmonds, Kathy Scott, Iris Loram and her mother Pat.

SECTION FOUR
Chard's Villages

Whitestaunton, near Chard, *c.*1909. The tiny hamlet to the west of Chard has altered little in the eighty years since this picture was taken.

Chardstock, 1910. Francis Edward Larcombe, who died from injuries sustained in the First World War, and his wife Emily make a charming family group with their five children, especially the young boys with their best suits and collars. All four boys – Francis junior at the rear, the twins, Edward and Albert, and Walter – all played cricket for Chardstock. The daughter, Matilda Charity, was soon drafted in as a tea lady.

Chardstock Club Fête, 1903. The band marches up the hill towards the Manor grounds accompanied by a young lady at the head who seems part of the proceedings, probably a fête queen.

Chardstock, 1925. This attractive group of girls is dressed for the village bazaar. Back, left to right: Flo Searle, Phylis Hutchings, Flossie Farrant, Lena Farrant. Front: Elsie Pearce, Jessie Dunster.

Chardstock Bazaar, 1925, held in the vicarage grounds. This lady's contribution seems to be mats, rugs and shawls, probably all handmade.

Chardstock Church Choir, 1930. Back row, left to right: John Pratt, William Beviss, Clifford Symes, Tom Parris, Bill Apsey, Albert Goff, Jack Strawbridge, Syd Goff, Mansfield Hayson (organist), George Harris, Harold Pratt, Walter Smith. Middle row: Arthur Apsey, Alb Harris, Bill Brownsell, Owen Case, Harry Shears, Bob Hutchings, Charles Strawbridge. Front row: Jessie Perring, Mrs Pearce, Evelyn Pratt, Phylis Hutchings, Miss White, Revd Albert Joscelyne (vicar 1919-30), Mrs Joscelyne, Mrs A. Hayson, Ella Pearce, Mrs Symes.

Chard Show, 1958. Sheila Martin of Tatworth Fruit Farm shows off some of the produce to some young visitors.

South Chard Strict Baptist chapel stone-laying, 9 April 1909. Five stones were laid at the ceremony, one by each of three deacons, one by the oldest member of the congregation present and one, the first, by the pastor Mr Thomas Dare. Under the first stone was placed a bottle containing particulars of the cause and the erection of the new chapel, a copy of the articles of faith of the Gospel Standard Society, a *Gospel Standard* and a *Friendly Companion* for that April. The site cost £60, the building £600-700.

The finished chapel, which is still is use today.

Tatworth School, 1914. The teacher, Miss Ethel Hoare, came back into teaching as Mrs Bishop during the Second World War and taught the children of many of those she had taught in the First World War.

Tatworth School Sports Day, 1950. Back row, left to right: Roy Guppy, Pat Bilyard, Tony Lillington, Gerald Culverwell, Keith Broughton, Derek Loosemore, Robert Hawker, Ivor Down. Front row: Mike Passmore, Ann Kettle, Wendy Hounsell, Enice Scott, Heather Dowell, Jean Martin, Jean Jenkins, Alan Board.

Chard Junction, seen here around 1908, was opened by the LSWR on 19 July 1860 as Chard Road but changed its name to Chard Junction in August 1872. The branch line to Chard is on the left, the main Waterloo–Exeter line is behind the sheds on the right. Although Beeching closed the branch line to passengers on 8 September 1962 and goods traffic ended about four years later, the junction itself stayed open until 7 March 1967 to cater for the nearby milk factory's trade.

Chard Junction, 1914. It is surprising how paranoid officialdom becomes in time of war. Soon after the outbreak of the First World War these five members of the Somerset Light Infantry, including Corporal Albert Farrant from Chardstock, were guarding Chard Junction against invasion and saboteurs.

Tatworth Special Constables, 1942. Scrumping apples, a time-honoured pastime for country boys, must have become a forgotten art during the war with so many long arms of the law around. The group includes Howard Woolcott, Vic Paull, Fred Board, Lloyd Staples and local bobby PC 'Tiny' Weaver at the rear.

The Fowler brothers from Tatworth all served in the forces in the Second World War and all six came home. Back, left to right: Bill, Walter, Bob, Fred. Front: Roland, Harold.

Tatworth School, c.1920. The introduction of compulsory education, one of the nine-teenth century's boons for small rural communities, led to the opening of Tatworth School in 1879. The long-serving Frank Puddicombe was headmaster at the time of this picture. The school is still open.

Tatworth post office, c.1930.

Belle View Terrace, South Chard, *c.*1908. Tatworth School is in the background.

Tatworth School, 1966. The helpers who built the swimming pool pose beside their hand-iwork at the official opening. Left to right: Don Down, Hedley Morgan, Ken Hawker, Fred Mitchell, Mr Weeks (headmaster), Les Legge, Maurice Duke, Geoff Meech, Eric Samways, John Cockram, Frank Bullen, -?-, -?-, -?-.

Alice 'Granny' Beer of Winsham. Mrs Beer, who died in 1959 aged 93, *was* the village. The mother of sixteen children, she assisted as unofficial midwife at the birth of half the children in Winsham during her adult life.

Church Street, Winsham, *c.*1905. Just what part the retail trade played in the economy of a town or village can be seen by the fact that Holcombe's stores, later Appleby's, had a shop staff of four, an odd-job man, and a 'delivery boy' beside the van from which he sold direct to the public. The horse was stabled behind the shop. The Kings Arms next door also had stables at the rear. The tall building on the front left is the Jubilee Hall.

The Loaring family, Winsham, *c.*1900. The Loarings, still represented in the village today, are Winsham's oldest family, mentioned in the church registers as early as 1561 and going back even further than that. Thomas Malachi Loaring poses at the turn of the century with his wife, Ellen Rosa, and other members of the family, including his four sons.

Winsham School. Mr Southcombe's class in 1906.

Church Street, Winsham, *c.*1904. Most Edwardian postcard photographers attracted the locals, especially the children. But this is such a well-dressed group it is hard to dismiss the notion they have been asked to pose outside St Stephen's church. The third building on the right was Daisy Boait's bakehouse, and beyond it was the Bell, from where customers would need to be careful to avoid the open ditch on dark nights. It has long since been filled in. Once there were four inns in the village; today the Bell is the sole survivor.

Fore Street, Winsham, *c.*1904, probably taken at the same time as the picture above. The children look like those in Church Street.

Thorncombe celebrations for George V's coronation, 1911.

Thorncombe Home Guard outside the Jubilee Hall about 1942. The machine-gunners are K. Champion, H. French, J. Sutton, J. Saunders, A. Ball and R. Larcombe.

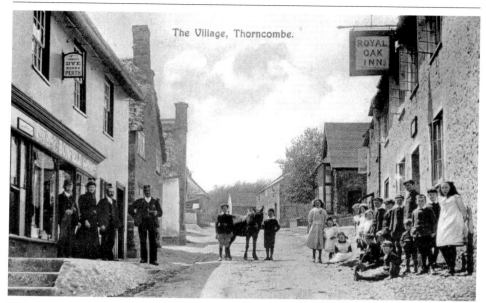

The Village, Thorncombe.

Thorncombe was transferred from Devon to Dorset in 1846 when the boundaries between the two counties and those with Somerset were tidied up. However, Thorncombe has a Chard postal address and its mail at the time of this picture (c.1910) would have come from there to the post office at Bondfield's on the left. The Royal Oak (right) has long since been closed.

Thorncombe, c.1900. A load of corn and a cart try to pass on what looks like a sea of mud.

Winsham School infants' class, 1938. Among the pupils are Jean and Mary Beer, Betty Long, Norman Phelps, Helen Hyde and Mary Crandon.

Owsley's Bakehouse, Wadeford, near Chard, c.1900. Mr Owsley's open cart might not find favour with modern health inspectors, but the sight of the crusty cottage loaves will bring a whiff of nostalgia to those who can remember 'real' bread. Mr Owsley is in the middle, his son in the delivery cart to the left.

Chard & District Co-op, Wadeford, *c.*1910. A private residence since closing in the 1960s, Wadeford's Co-op stood on the site of an old smithy. Owsley's Bakehouse is to the right; Mr Pavey the wheelwright lived on the left. The building behind was Powderloon cloth mill. It became the youth club and is a private house today.

Wadeford, near Chard, *c.*1910. The Rising Sun on the left is today's Haymaker Inn. The building behind the car vanished long ago when the road was widened. Opposite is Long's grocery shop. One of the first motor cycles here is propped against the wall of the pub.

Combe St Nicholas, *c.*1902. The local Methodists, banners flying and band playing, march down from their church hidden behind the post office. The occasion was enough to bring out two policemen. The post office is still there but, sadly, the George has closed.

Combe St Nicholas, *c.*1900. The High Street outside St Nicholas's church and the George.

The village green, Combe St Nicholas, *c.*1908. The lamp standard was erected for Queen Victoria's Diamond Jubilee in 1897.

Combe St Nicholas, *c*.1950. Revd William Thomas Taylor MBE hands presents to Mrs Long on her retirement as church caretaker. Mr Taylor, who died in office, was a much loved vicar from 1946 to 1982.

The post office, Bishopswood, *c*.1933. Although there has not been much change to the actual building, considerable development has taken place below.

Mr and Mrs Every, *c.*1884. Mr J. Every was postmaster at Buckland St Mary for fifty-five years from 1874 to 1929.

Buckland St Mary post office, *c.*1904. The postmaster, Mr J. Every, is standing in the entrance.

Eagle Tavern, Buckland St Mary, *c.*1910. W. Collins of Newtown poses outside the popular tavern on the main London road. Charles Collins and Walter Snook are to his left.

Lamb and Flag Inn, Buckland St Mary, *c.*1900. A rare old picture taken before the inn was practically rebuilt.

Buckland St Mary, 17 April 1911. A triple wedding, the groups posing outside St Mary's church. The happy couples are, left to right: Robert Podbury and Ellen Shire, George White and Laura Elsie Diment, and Edwin Matravers and Ette Jane Tutcher.

Buckland St Mary, c.1900. One of the first motor cars seen in the village. The driver is thought to be the Bishop of Bath and Wells on a visit to a fête in the vicarage grounds. The vicar, Revd Arthur Porcher Lance, is probably the person with his back to the camera.

Buckland St Mary School, 1928. Back row, left to right: Harold Jenkins, Harold Dyer, Jim Collins, Gordon Dyer, Ken Gready, Roy Quick. Middle row: Reg White, Henry Mutter, Arthur Grabham, Roy Mutter, Hubert Dyer, Ivor Mutter, Fred Dymond, Raymond White. Front row: Ivy Buttle, Peggy Collins, Vera Powers, Stella Grabham, Edie Pedon, Kathleen Grabham.

Buckland St Mary School, c.1905.

Buckland St Mary, *c.*1909. Buckland stands some 700 feet up in the Blackdown Hills with staggering views in all directions. In the right background is the village school which was built with stone similar to the grey stone used in the construction of St Mary's church.

Buckland St Mary, 1902. One woman and her dog outside the church survey the decorations for Edward VII's coronation.

Little Hill Farm, Buckland St Mary, *c*.1923. This mid-village farm has changed little since the picture was taken. Mr and Mrs Clark pose with the baby, Ken Gready. The lady to the right is Mrs Sam Gready.

Buckland St Mary, *c*.1900. The Lamb and Flag after its renovation (see pp. 45 and 114). The balcony has long since been removed.

Ilminster Within

North Street, Ilminster, *c.*1904. The old post office is to the right. London House is now the local branch of Lloyds Bank.

Ditton Street, Ilminster, *c.*1950. Despite the two parked cars, traffic was not a problem in those days for the Taunton Vale Hunt, led by huntsman Jim Bailey through narrow Ditton Street after meeting in the Square.

E.J. Baker & Sons, Ditton Street, Ilminster, 1953. Edwin Baker began his bakery business in Ditton Street in 1909, trading there until his death in 1960. Two years later his sons sold the business. This part of Ilminster has always been prone to flooding.

Ilminster Sports, *c.*1906. A close finish in what appears to be a two-boy race in the sports held beside the Lamb Inn at Horton Cross.

Ilminster Shooting Club, *c.*1901. The unusual thing about this picture is not only that the ladies make up most of the audience, but that they also engage in the far from genteel sport of shooting.

Ilminster Hospital Carnival, 1922. Olive Clark, also a collector, and John Clapp, two entrants in the walking classes.

E.J. Baker & Sons, Ditton Street, Ilminster, 1950. The bakehouse was behind the shop in Shudrick Lane. Edwin Baker on the left is seen with one of his sons, Cyril, and his brother Charlie (right), with some of the Christmas cakes. Sugar was still rationed at the time so the sides of the cakes are un-iced.

Winners of the Somerset Wing Cup in 1966 were 2381 Squadron (Ilminster) ATC. Back row, left to right: Paul Smyth, Graham Cave, Graham Whaites, Graham Trott, Michael Hemsley, Des Bulpin, Keith Penny. Front row: Clive Hemsley, Peter Tolley, Wg/Cdr. Winn, Fl.Lt. Bowery, Richard Crockett, Neil Raffel.

Ilminster Grammar School, c.1908. Mr Mermagen was headmaster at the time, having just arrived from a similar post at Colyton Grammar School. The school was founded in 1549 in buildings next to St Mary's churchyard in the town centre, moving to its present home in 1874. It was closed as a grammar school in 1971 and, following a spell as a comprehensive school, is today the Greenfylde Primary School catering for the 5-9 years age group.

Ilminster Grammar School Cadet Force, 1922. The NCOs are top heavy with four sergeants to just one corporal.

Ilminster Grammar School, 1924. Games master F.S. Carpenter poses with the cricket 1st XI. Fred Carpenter was appointed second master in 1922, acting as games master and taking Scripture and History. He acted as headmaster during Mr Robert Graham's absence on war service, 1940-2. He had been at the school for forty-three years when he died in service in 1965, shortly before he was due to retire.

Ilminster Grammar School soccer 1st XI, 1949. Back row, left to right: Dibble (linesman), John Keate, Edgar Male, -?-, John Hunt, Jim Crow, Don Lawrence, Frederick Carpenter. Front row: Alan Brown, Cecil Gale, Clive Reeves, Richard Maddocks (capt.), Arnold Trott, Mickey Cake, John England.

Ilminster Square, c.1875, one of the earliest views of Ilminster, looking towards East Street. Points of interest are the buildings towards the rear on the right since pulled down; the site now houses the Nat West Bank. Just visible outside the shop on the right immediately past Ditton Street is a shovel – for collecting horse droppings!

Ilminster post office, 1916. The tall building to the right was built to replace an old building destroyed by fire in January 1915. It was built by W.A. Hutchings as offices and warehouse for Messrs J. & G. Taylor. The front is of artificial stone resembling the local Ham stone., which was made locally at Ilminster's Wharf Lane works.

QUEEN VICTORIA
Stopped here one night,
23. December 1819,
this Hotel being the first
at which she ever stayed,

George Hotel, Ilminster, c.1911. As the postcard's caption tells us, the George, a fine old coaching inn in Ilminster's Square, was the first hotel Queen Victoria ever stayed in. She stopped there on the night of 23 December 1819 with her parents the Duke and Duchess of Kent. The following night they were in Sidmouth, where the Duke had gone to escape his many creditors. He died there in January.

The Square, Ilminster, 1904. One of Ilminster's earliest cars is outside the Wilts and Dorset bank, now Lloyds. Besides the car, three other forms of transport can be seen: carriage, foot and bicycle.

Silver Street, Ilminster, c.1905. Wheadons, in Leicester House, has become R.A. Dyer, but this part of the town, opposite St Mary's church, has hardly changed.

Lord and Lady Poulett at the ceremony when Lady Poulett laid the foundation stone of the new village hall at Allowenshay near Ilminster around 1916.

Broadway Congregational church, near Ilminster, *c.*1905.

Ilminster Burma Star Association was formed in 1952 with over fifty members, three of whom are still serving including the first chairman, Reg Hopkins, who is now president. Members pictured here on a trip to Exmouth around 1957 are, standing, left to right: Albert Perry, Reg Hopkins, Ernie Tolman, Walter Clarke, Herbie Lee, Ken Carbin, Harold Court, Major General Woods, Bill Male, Dave Whitfield, Ron Rodford, William Benjafield, Harry Burton, -?-. Sitting: Jimmy Aplin, Cyril Davies, Jack Marshalsea, Trevor Reid, George Moore, Mervyn Canniford.

Ilminster Town Football Club, 1946/7. The trophies on show are the Perry Street Charity Cup, Somerset Charity Cup, Chard British Legion Cup, Crewkerne Hospital Cup and the Perry Street League. Back row, left to right: A. Dade, R. Marks (secretary), W. Paull (trainer), H. Dyte, E. Thresher, K. Perry, R. Churchill, M. Sibley (capt.), L. Clarke, J. Crossman, G. Clarke, W. Sibley, L. Greer, A. Duke, L. Clapp. Front row: Preb. G.C. Hickman (president), G. Simpson, V. Woodhall, G. White, D. Harris, M. Thresher, F.W. Abbott (chairman).

Ilminster Thursday Football Club, 1930/1. The white towel for the trainer was a compulsory part of the team photograph in those days.

West Street, Ilminster, 1918. The residential part of the town with the spire of the new Weslyan church plainly visible in the background. Hurlstone's on the right was a cycle shop.

Ilminster Sunday School outing, 1908. The procession moves past the junction of West Street and Station Road. The central house on the right has since been taken down to make way for the road to Summerlands.

Ilminster Mixed Hockey Team, c.1908.

Ilminster Carnival. The 'Sue Sue Band' entry in the 1932 walking classes. Note the poster behind offering 'Cunard to Canada' reductions from £3 to £2.

Ilminster Town Football Club, 1938/9, arguably the best team ever to play in the Perry Street & District Football League, certainly the most successful, with no less than eight trophies – the Ilminster Charity Cup, Chard Hospital Cup, Perry Street League Champions Cup, Somerset Charity Cup, Crewkerne Hospital Cup, Perry Street Charity Cup, Ilminster Carnival Cup and Somerset Junior Cup – on view. Axminster Town (1919/22) and Stoke-under-Ham (1934/8) may have have had longer reigns at the top, but there is no telling what Ilminster might have done if the Second World War had not intervened. To round off this season, the side played twenty games, including two semi-finals and four finals, in twenty-eight days. They won fifteen, drew two and lost three of the games, two of the defeats coming when they played two games on the same day, and one of those after a cup final when the title was already safely theirs. To any survivor of their considerable following of those days this line-up must sound like the authentic muster call of the gods. Back row, left to right: F.W. Abbott, J. Gear, W. Paull, R. Sibley, P. Hext, K. Sibley, D. Trott, M. Sibley, D. Coombes, R. Marks, A. Duke. Front row: A. Chick, G. White, A. Marks, D. Wade, V. Woodhall, W. Miller, G. Clarke.

Ilminster School treat in East Street, *c.*1909.

East Street, Ilminster, *c.*1910. Batten & Coombes, gents' outfitters, now the post office, have a natty line in straw hats and are agents for Aertex.

Ilminster Boys' Brigade, *c.*1905, parading through the Triangle at West Street outside Hayman's shop.

Robey Mission Hall, Shudrick Street, *c.*1910. The spire has been taken down, the railings went in the Second World War for salvage, and today the building is used as a garage.

Hayman's Steam Bakery, West Street, Ilminster, *c.*1904. The Hayman family baking business celebrated its centenary in 1991, John George Hayman, who fell in love with the trade when he was a baker in the Royal Navy in the last century, settling at Wheelwright House, Ilton in 1891. He later bought Bullens Farm in the village, where he combined farming with a bakery already in existence at the farmhouse (see p. 158). His son Frederick, on the left in this picture, operated the business in West Street in premises known to this day as Tolley's Old Bakery. When John George died in 1919, Frederick sold the West Street bakery, moving to Ilton to carry on the family business. By the early 1930s business had expanded enough for a new bakery, still in use today albeit modernized, to be built in the orchard behind Bullens Farm. The third Hayman generation, Frederick's sons Leslie and Norman, ran the business until 1965. Leslie's son Tim and his wife Jenny, the fourth generation, bought the business and expanded it, opening a shop in Holyrood Street, Chard in 1973, later moving along the street to bigger premises. In 1974 they opened a second shop in Ilminster's Silver Street. Today the fifth generation of the family, Claire, works just a few yards from where her great great grandfather transferred his bakery early this century, and her highly professional cake decorating would have brought a proud smile to old John George's face.

Ilminster Show's officers and judges, c.1904.

Ilminster Cycling Club outside the Wesleyan chapel in West Street, c.1905. The club's HQ was at the George Hotel and it was a flourishing organization in the late nineteenth and early twentieth centuries. The two gentlemen on the left are the Keitch brothers.

Ilminster Tennis Club, c.1957. Back row, left to right: George Maher, Nancy Dyer, -?- (behind), Judy Gould, Eileen Maher, Michael Richards and Peter Bishop (behind), -?-, Gladys Burbidge, Mrs Pike, -?-, Brian Lacey, George Burbidge, John Pike, Geoff Morgan, Brian Sparkes, Desmond Broom. Sitting: Pat Maher, Margaret Cooper, Linda Burbidge, Janet Hawkes, June Hawkes.

Ilminster Cricket Club vs Somerset, Harold Gimblett's Testimonial, 1948. Back row, left to right: George Trump (umpire), Fred Dolman, A. Harris, Arnold Trott, ? Crockett, George Tarr, Ike Sawyer, Fred Carpenter (umpire). Front row: R. Stoman, Bryn Mattravers, George Davey, F. Harvey, -?-, J. Welch.

Pat Saunders at Ilminster Carnival in the early 1950s. Later, as Mrs Pat Hooper, she was a founder member of the Ilminster Harlequins Carnival Club whose tableaux met with such success on the local carnival circuit in the 1980s.

Broadway Fête, *c.*1910.

F.T. Adams's grocery shop at the top of East Street, 1908. Mr Adams is seen with his grand daughter Edith.

A procession for an unknown occasion makes its way along East Street.

Ilminster Brewery owner Colonel J.R. Paull's residence in Brewery Lane in 1905, since converted to flats.

Ilminster station, seen here shortly before its closure on 8 September 1962, was opened ninety-six years earlier on 11 September 1866. Apart from one minor alteration its layout remained unchanged throughout its working life, after which it was declared a listed building.

Station Road, Ilminster, c.1909.

Further along Station Road, c.1930. The Railway Hotel on the left is now the Lord Nelson. The 'B' of Bradford & Sons, coal and builders merchants, is just visible on the right.

Looking down North Street, Ilminster, c.1910. Haycrafts General Stores is on the left; below, but out of sight on the right, is the George Hotel. A special occasion, possibly George V's coronation, has brought out the crowd.

Jordans, Ilminster, c.1920. The home of the Speke family, Jordans became a private school before being demolished to make room for development in the 1960s.

SECTION SIX

Ilminster Without

JORDANS' FETE, 1906.

The balloon goes up at Jordans, near Ilminster, a popular venue for shows and fêtes. This one, held in 1906, was probably the Conservative Fête.

Another fête at Jordans in 1909. An unknown attraction (the return of the balloon seen on p. 145?) is the centre of attention.

Whitelackington Forge, *c*.1910, later burnt down and rebuilt. Whitelackington was the main home of the Speke family in the seventeenth century, and it was there that they were visited by the Duke of Monmouth in 1680. Later, in 1685, Charles Speke was condemned by Judge Jeffreys merely for having shaken hands with Monmouth and was hanged in Ilminster Square.

Whitelackington Cricket Club, *c*.1930. Members of the team include Harold Male, Eddie Scott, Jack Holtom, Bill Sphinx, 'Shep' Wyatt, the local shepherd, and Harold Harris, the scorer.

Stocklinch, near Ilminster, *c*.1906.

Dowlish Wake, *c.*1909. Trust the boys to stand in the water. The great explorer Captain John Hanning Speke, discover of Lake Tanganyika, Lake Victoria and the source of the Nile, is buried in St Andrew's church in the village.

Broadway Congregational church, *c.*1908, now a private residence. The war memorial on the left was blown over in the tremendous gales that swept the area in January 1990.

Broadway Ringers, 1905. Left to right: Mr Denman, Mr Hodges, the curate (behind), Frank Welch, Bill Warry.

Ashill, c.1910. Judging by the well-dressed girls and the men in the carriage wearing their best suits, this was almost certainly taken on a Sunday.

Horton Schoolhouse, *c.*1905. Today it is a private house and the school seen behind has been converted to flats. Once on the busy A303 trunk road to the West Country, Horton has been changed back to a quiet rural community by the Ilminster bypass.

Horton Wesleyan chapel, *c.*1906. The chapel is still in use but the blacksmiths shop to the left has disappeared.

Horton Rovers Football Club, October 1910. A founder member of the Perry Street & District League, Horton, unlike many village teams of the time, are turned out in identical kit, including even the goalkeeper, with cap at rear. Back row, left to right: -?-, C. Raffell, F. Gulliford, T. Bishop, W. Dack, A. Bishop, W. Adams, H. Stone, T. Hopkins, J.A. Small, H.R. Morris, J. Parsons.

Haymaking at Hastings Farm, Ilton, c.1918. Andrew Yarde is fifth left. It is easy to see how much the farmer once depended on real 'horse power' when you consider the size of the load that one horse has just brought to the rick yard.

Ashill post office, *c.*1914. The post office had been next to the school and later moved back there. Today it is at the village crossroads.

Haymaking at Hastings Farm, Ashill, *c.*1920. Another good example of the work that a farm horse got through. Winnie, Charles and Bob Ottery are 'helping' their father. The head on the top of the load belongs to Charles Kinglake, and Mr Ottery is on the right.

Hastings Farm, Ashill, *c.*1900. Mr and Mrs Andrew Yarde with their daughters, the future Mrs W. Matravers and Mrs D. Crabbe.

Ashill School, *c.*1910. The school, which has been enlarged, still serves the community.

Haymaking at Hastings Farm, *c.*1920. Included in the group are Fred Trump, third left, 'Whisky' Perry, on his left, Wally Matravers, third right, and Charles Kinglake, on his left.

Donyalt Halt, pictured here soon after its closure on 8 September 1962, was a mile to the south of Ilminster station on the Taunton–Chard branch line. It was opened on 5 May 1928 and had a single platform edged with sleepers and a small wooden shelter which, like many such local railway sheds, was built by Harry Hebditch of Martock.

Ilton Methodist church, c.1909. Ilton, a Saxon settlement, derives its name from its position near to the River Isle. It was the home of Sir Nicholas Wadham (1561–1609) who, with his wife Dorothy, founded Wadham College, Oxford.

Ilton Halt, seen here in 1960, was opened on 26 May 1928 and, although comfortable enough once you were on the platform, access was by means of a narrow, often muddy path. Like the rest of the Chard branch it fell foul of Dr Beeching in September 1962.

Ilton School group, *c.*1905.

Ilton Fête, 18 July 1907, probably held in a field beside the Wyndham Arms. This shows the extent to which the reasonably new-fangled bicycle had become an everyday asset for the working classes.

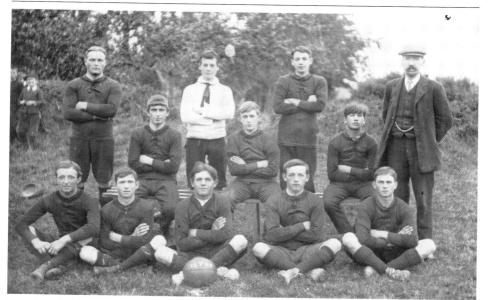

Ilton Football Club, *c.*1908.

Ilton Fête, 1907. The men are acting as models in a best decorated hat competition but few seem to be happy about it.

Hayman's Bakery, Ilton, *c*.1900. The fifth generation of the Hayman family is currently working for this 101-year-old business (see p. 137).

Ilminster Cycling Club pictured outside the Hatch Inn at Hatch Beauchamp, 1912. The members are probably enjoying an outing to William Jennings's pub; they would hardly be on a spin with the ladies dressed like this.

Stocklinch Show and Races, 8 August 1907. Two of the entries in the decorated bicycle class.

Windwhistle Hotel, *c*.1930, now the Windwhistle Inn. The pub stands beside Chard's Windwhistle Golf Course and legend has it that the ghosts of smugglers and excise men chase each other outside exchanging ghostly shots. The road runs on towards Crewkerne which, with its neighbouring Ham stone villages, such as Merriott, Shepton Beauchamp, South Petherton and Stoke-sub-Hamdon, will be the subject of a forthcoming book.

Acknowledgements

We are grateful to all those who not only lent us pictures for this book but also gave up their time to talk about them. Our thanks go especially to Jeff Farley of Chard for pictures from his fine collection and for his introduction, and to Vic Matravers of Ashill for access to his collection of material on Ilminster and the surrounding villages. Thanks also to Isla Baker, Helwyn Bass, Peter Baulch, Derek Best, Peter Beviss, Allan Brown, Syd Cane, Kevin Clancy, Sheila Chilver, Jill Colledge, Maurice Cunnold, Geraldine Dennis, Jennifer Hayman, Jean Hyde, Thomas Jennings, Betty Keate, Mary Loaring, Albert Manley, Helen Meech, Geoff Palmer, Gilbert Spurdle, John Stevens, Ann Sweetland and Syd Tolley. Our thanks also to Friend Bowers for patiently answering our questions, to Keith Fountaine for help with the pictures on p. 15 and p. 16, to Violet Gosling, who allowed her front room to become a store for boxes of pictures, and to Haydon Wood, editor of *Pulmans Weekly News,* for technical assistance.